Penguin Handbooks
Children Growing Up

CW00330595

Eurfron Gwynne Jones is a zoology graduate of
University College, Cardiff, where she also received
her doctorate in zoology in 1959. After leaving
university she joined the B.B.C., working first in
radio and then in television, where she was
responsible for producing science programmes for
schools. She is now a Senior Producer in the
Further Education Department of B.B.C. television
and is responsible for programmes in the areas of
child development and human relations. Among her
recent series are *Expecting A Baby*, *Children
Growing Up* (on which this book is based) and
Parents and Children.

Eurfron Gwynne Jones
Children Growing Up

Penguin Books

Penguin Books Ltd, Harmondsworth,
Middlesex, England
Penguin Books Inc., 7110 Ambassador Road,
Baltimore, Maryland 21207, USA.
Penguin Books Australia Ltd, Ringwood,
Victoria, Australia

Published in Penguin Books 1973
Copyright © Eurfron Gwynne Jones, 1973
Designed by Veronica Loveless

Filmset in Photon Times by
Richard Clay (The Chaucer Press), Ltd, Bungay,
Suffolk, and printed in Great Britain by
Fletcher & Son, Ltd, Norwich

To Michael

Contents

Acknowledgements

This book is based on the BBC film series 'Children Growing Up'. The photographs were taken by the production team during the filming.

E.G.J.

Introduction

Children do not just grow – they are 'brought up'. In this book I have tried to show how parents can and do influence the kind of person their child will become.

A child who has never been spoken to or heard language will not automatically start to speak, and a child who is not given the freedom and opportunity to play and explore his surroundings will not reach his full potential of understanding. Even more important, a child who in his early years is not loved may not find it easy to develop satisfactory relationships when he is older.

This book looks at five main areas of development – the changing relationship between mother and child, the development of the child's understanding of the world around him, physical growth, the growth of language and, finally, the way all these things come together and are expressed in the changing pattern of play.

The parents and children described come from a wide range of backgrounds – social, cultural and educational. And where a point is illustrated by a specific child it is based on observation and research carried out with large numbers of children by people involved in all aspects of child development.

The book is based on a series of films I produced for BBC Television called *Children Growing Up*. In this series I aimed to capture on film the behaviour of children from birth to five years and to do this in their own homes and families. Each chapter follows the pattern of one programme in the series and covers one aspect of development, such as language, which is then traced through from birth to five years. The purpose of this approach was to make it easier for parents watching the series to understand the development of their own children and to recognize, and perhaps avoid, some of the pitfalls. The same aims and approach apply to this book.

Making the Films

One of my first problems in filming children in their family surroundings was the whole paraphernalia of filming. How do you get half a dozen bulky men, two women, a camera, tape recorder and microphone and some rather glaring lights into a kitchen? And furthermore, assuming you can get them in, how do you prevent them influencing the behaviour of the family? The answer is of course that you can never avoid influencing the situation, but there are ways of reducing the influence to a minimum. First of all when you include adults in the filming you can make sure they have more on their minds than a film crew! If a mother is preparing a meal for three hungry boys she doesn't have much chance to be self-conscious about it – the milk boils over, one of the boys starts hitting his brother, the cat gets under her feet. It is no wonder she shouts at them and slams the oven door. Similarly at bath time no mother is going to be worried about presenting her best profile to camera at the expense of a soapy, slithery three-month-old.

Equally, if you are concentrating on a child during the filming then you need to give him more interesting things to look at than the film crew. If a child is visiting a zoo for the first time it takes a very odd-looking film crew indeed to compete for attention with the antics of the monkeys. Even a supermarket is full of more interesting things than a camera: other children being pushed around in wire 'prams', booming announcements over the loud speaker, rows upon rows of different colours and shapes. A film crew is lost in all this.

Nevertheless, children are still influenced to some extent by the presence of a film crew – though this gave me an added insight into their different stages of development. The older the children were, the more effect we seemed to have on their behaviour. With very young

babies there is no problem except the physical one of keeping strong lights out of their eyes, and not frightening them with too much noise. With older babies who were not yet walking we found we were very quickly 'outside their world'. When we filmed two thirteen-month-olds – Willy and Catherine – they crawled around in the centre of the room, stopping occasionally to wrestle together with some toy that caught their attention. Occasionally they strayed quite close to the camera and once or twice rolled practically into the lens. When this happened they stared hard at it for a second or two and then crawled back into their own circle. We were all gathered in the corner of the room and I could almost see the boundary which separated their world from ours. Children of this age pay attention only to the things that happen quite close to them – anything further away does not seem to act on their senses and is ignored.

We filmed Catherine on many occasions from one year to three years and watched her attitude towards us change. Far from becoming easier to film each time, it became more difficult the more she got used to us. As she grew older she became more conscious of us, more curious about what we were doing, and, occasionally, she was deliberately uncooperative when she resented our intrusion. Once, when I wanted to film her playing 'tea parties' with her Teddy and dolls, I made the mistake of producing some real sweets. She spent the rest of the afternoon hiding them in all corners of the room, behind Teddy's ear and in the cameraman's pocket. She had found the perfect diversion and skilfully sabotaged our afternoon's work.

When Catherine was about two she also became more aware of and more curious about our gadgetry. When we were anxious to pick up what small children were saying we fitted them with radio microphones. These allow the children freedom to wander anywhere and still be recorded. The arrangement has one drawback – a short piece of wire dangles from the transmitter – this is the aerial. The two-year-old Catherine found this irresistible – and of course the more we tried to stop her playing with it the more determined she became. The crackles and squeaks on the sound tape every time she fiddled with it nearly resulted in another lost day.

Older children – those between three and a half and five – posed other problems. They seemed to fall into three main categories:

(a) those who were very self-conscious and hid from us or froze;

(b) those who never forgot our presence and performed specifically for us; and

(c) those who genuinely became absorbed in what they were doing and quickly forgot us.

We soon learned to recognize and concentrate on the third group.

It was usually towards the end of the filming, when we were after specific situations, that our problems were greatest. In the early days we filmed just about everything that happened. Gradually as the programmes took shape we found there were gaps that needed filling. Fathers formed one of these gaps, mainly because they are never around during the day when children are active. I shall not forget the day we tried to do something about this. We were filming a family of three boys. The normal schedule of their late afternoon is watching *Playschool*, tea-time and then when Daddy arrives a rough and tumble followed by a bedtime story.

To make sure of this sequence we arranged that Daddy should come home earlier than usual and we would film the welcome he got on his arrival. Unfortunately he was a little too early and his arrival coincided with *Playschool*. From the point of view of the sequence we were trying to get, the result was disastrous. At first he was totally ignored and then when I turned off the television their absorption erupted into screams and tears with Daddy obviously held responsible.

Those were some of the problems of the filming itself. Afterwards came the problem of structuring the material to make the best use of 70,000 ft (about fourteen miles) of film. The pattern I finally chose is the one followed in this book.

The Relationship Between
Mother and Child

Food, clothes, shelter – these are the physical provisions a mother makes for her child. And this side of a mother's care remains fairly constant throughout childhood. The emotional side of the relationship on the other hand changes and develops as the child grows up. As the child starts to learn it is usually the mother who is there to encourage it. With her a child takes his first steps, learns his first words, makes his first discoveries about the world and learns his first limits of behaviour. Whether this is an exciting and enjoyable time for both of them, or a power struggle full of worry and tears, influences the progress the child makes and the kind of person he will become.

The learning takes place from the earliest weeks and it is two-sided. Mother and baby learn together. We saw this happening with Fiona and her mother.

It was in the premature baby unit of a hospital that we first met Fiona. She was born four weeks early. Her mother told us she had scarcely seen a baby before and was rather scared of looking after one all on her own. After a few weeks of visiting Fiona and being allowed to hold her, the time had come for her mother to take her home. Before this happened, a nurse showed Fiona's mother how to cope with breast feeding and bathing the baby. At home six weeks later Fiona's mother was more confident and enjoyed looking after her. At feeding time, Fiona fixed her eyes on her mother's face, made appreciative noises and smiled at the sound of her mother's voice encouraging her. At bath time her face showed signs of apprehension as she was lowered into the water — quickly changing to satisfaction and confidence as she felt the familiar arm supporting her. Even at nappy changing time there was a 'conversation' between them. Encouraging words, gestures and smiles from her mother. Kicks and cries of pleasure from the baby. Nobody had told Fiona's mother to behave like this, it was something she and most other mothers do instinctively. Fiona's pleasure and reactions stimulated her mother's attention and in turn her mother's response meant security to Fiona.

In these early weeks and months Fiona was hearing the sounds of what will become her language and seeing the expressions on her mother's face which she will come to associate with pleasure, amusement, anger and frustration. In time she will learn to respond to these with her own sounds and expressions. She is learning all the time.

As her body and limbs gain strength new skills will emerge and need encouragement. She will first reach out for things which catch her attention, then crawl after them and finally stagger on her own two feet. Her mother will progress to learning that praise reinforces the child's efforts and encouragement builds up her perseverance. When walking is mastered nothing in the house is safe up to a level of about 3 ft. Those things which are not tough enough to be chewed, dropped or banged together need to be put out of reach. Because the child has reached the peak of the age of exploration, nothing will be sacred. Now she will want to be involved in everything. During

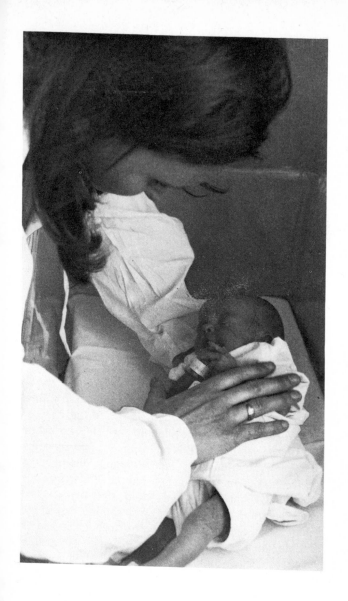

this time a mother has to find the happy medium by providing the kind of help which develops initiative but doesn't destroy interest.

All along the mother has been laying the groundwork for a child's development of language: now at about eighteen months she much more consciously becomes a language teacher. When children see new things they need to know the words for them. They may not use the words immediately, but they are all being stored away for use some time in the future. From an adult's reply to questions a child builds up an idea of the structure of language. Speaking to a child thus develops vocabulary and understanding.

There is one more field in which a mother is moulding what her child will become. From her a child learns what it should and should not do and whenever possible the reasons why and why not. This is the area where power struggles often develop because it is sometimes difficult in the heat of the moment to distinguish between the things we need to stop the child doing for his own safety and the things which we feel he should stop doing because they cause anxiety or embarrassment for us as adults.

We see examples of these power struggles occurring in many ways. Imagine a crowded waiting-room in a child welfare clinic. There's very little to keep the children amused except for one rocking horse which is the centre of many squabbles. Into this room comes a television film crew complete with lights, tape recorders, microphones and cameras. To any normal curious child it transforms the waiting-room into a new world. One five-year-old leaves the group and trots over to get a closer look at the camera. The cameraman has been expecting it and is quite prepared to show him how it works, but within seconds the child's mother seizes the boy by the arm and draws him away with a sharp slap and a 'Don't be nosey.' He really wasn't doing any harm, but he was drawing attention to himself and to her. By her rules this was not to be encouraged. But when curiosity is not encouraged it can wither and die and curiosity is a fundamental part of intelligence.

The next struggle takes place in a supermarket. A little girl about four years of age has wandered away from her mother down one of those aisles which must look like a kind of paradise to a four-year-old — biscuits, cakes, chocolates, lemonade, tins of all shapes and sizes. For a few minutes she is alone, but not unhappy. There's so much to take in. Now her mother appears, rushes down the aisle and delivers half a dozen hard slaps in a mixture of anger, anxiety and relief at the same time shouting: 'Don't you ever do that again.' The child clearly doesn't know what's hit her or what she was doing that was so wrong. As an adult looking on, it is easy to see both sides of the situation; as a parent involved in the scene, it is so easy to get things out of perspective.

For every power struggle there are fortunately many adult–child relationships of a more rewarding kind. One often hears mothers on a busy shopping expedition patiently answering a series of questions which would throw a professor.

'Mummy, why is that man singing?'

'Does his leg hurt?'

'Why doesn't he work like Daddy?'

'Why must we have a basket?'

Even in the freezing cold of a winter's day in the park many a mother waits patiently while a child pokes and prods at every leaf and puddle that catches the eye. These

mothers seem to realize instinctively that the child has a need to do this. It's not just mothers who make a contribution to a child's understanding. Fathers do it too in their own way – patiently demonstrating their tyre pressure gauges, foot pumps, battery chargers and a hundred and one other gadgets young children are curious about and want to learn how to use.

When this kind of concern for a child's need to find out is there, we usually take it for granted. It is when it is so obviously missing in parents that it stands out. Physical

deprivation is easy to spot and the remedy is straightforward. The kind of deprivation in which a child is discouraged at every turn is more subtle, but equally important in its effect.

The evidence for the effect of deprivation of love and interest on a child is of course not experimental evidence and never will be; but there are many studies of children living in institutions without the love and attention of one adult mother-figure which point strongly to the importance of the relationship between mother and child. Children from such institutions are often later than average in learning to speak, restrained in their play and curiosity and often have difficulty in forming stable relationships in later life. Where studies have been made of children living at home with their families, the attitude of the parents towards the child is the single most important factor governing development, and the importance of the parents' attitude begins in babyhood.

There are some unavoidable circumstances which can affect a mother–child relationship. One of these is the arrival of a new baby. The details may differ from one child to another but the general pattern of events in the following scene are very common. Willy was eighteen months old when his baby sister Jessica was born. Most of the time he is affectionate towards her – smothering her with hugs and kisses. But occasionally he responds differently. When the baby is obviously the centre of not only his mother's attention but also that of everyone else in the room, he doesn't like it. Catherine, *his* playmate, is finding Jessica irresistible and stands staring at the baby's tiny feet and toes wondering whether she can touch. Willy sits across the room looking at this. Then he moves in. First he tries to climb on his mother's knee, this proves difficult because the baby is already there, next he catches hold of the baby's foot and squeezes it so hard that she starts to cry. Finally he grabs Catherine by the arm and pulls her away. All this time he has his thumb in his mouth. His mother told me that thumb sucking was something he had given up, but returned to after Jessica was born. Also he would no longer climb the stairs alone, although he could do it before she was born. These were two outward signs of Willy's regression to babyhood which his mother recognized and understood. Recognizing the signs of the effect of a new baby on the first child

goes a long way towards not letting the jealousy get out of hand. Of course, preparing the child for the arrival of a new baby is the first step to lessening the jealousy. When it is unrecognized and therefore unconsciously provoked it can have a lasting effect on the relationship between the mother and the child.

Separation of a young child from its mother is another common source of disturbance, such as when a child goes into hospital. The effect of this event can be minimized by special care and consideration on the part of parents and hospital authorities. There are many ways in which this is already being done. The National Association for the

Welfare of Children in Hospital (NAWCH), with the
cooperation of some hospital staff, has worked hard to
get unrestricted visiting allowed in all children's hospitals
and wards. In areas where this has been checked, about
three quarters of the hospitals now allow this. Where
buildings and space allow, some hospitals permit mothers
to live in. They have their own cubicles and are able to be
with and help in the care of the child during its stay in
hospital. So far only a quarter of the hospitals in areas
investigated have this arrangement. Recently the Department of Health and Social Security has recommended
that all hospitals should provide these facilities and that
where possible families should be encouraged to have
their child at home during weekends and holidays. Although more hospitals now are recognizing the need for
arrangements like this, many are still against it in practice. If this still applies in your area the nearest
NAWCH group would be worth contacting for advice.

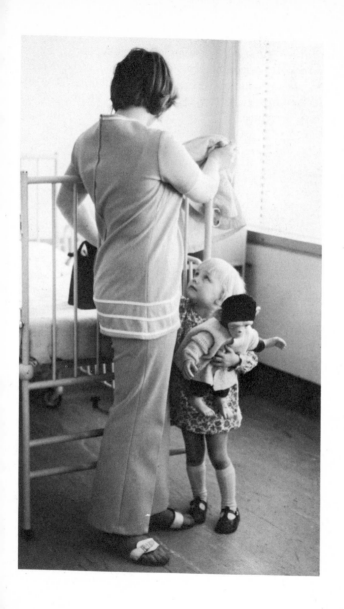

The move towards permitting parents to be with children in hospital is stimulated and supported by the work of a number of people who have studied the effect of an unhappy hospital experience on children. They describe three stages of response in young children – protest; detachment; despair. A child who is protesting

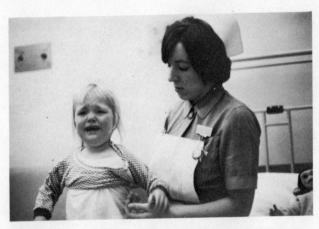

leaves no one in any doubt. Tears and tantrums are obvious enough. Detachment and despair are harder to recognize. When at visiting time a child ignores his parents, doesn't look at them or speak to them, he is showing the signs of detachment. Often by the end of visiting his

detachment disappears and he responds normally again. Then he is left once more. Despair can be the result of such experiences. Often it is misinterpreted as 'settling down' when the child is not crying or protesting any more. Just because a child is not giving any trouble it doesn't mean he is happy. A better sign of settling down is that he is responding to the other children and adults around him and playing with them when he is well enough. This is not meant to be a prophecy of doom for every child who has to go to hospital, but rather to draw attention to it as a potentially difficult time.

What can parents do? First of all where there is un-restricted visiting one or the other should try to be there at bedtime, when the child may feel particularly lost. Secondly, when a child is old enough to understand, parents should explain that they are leaving and when

they will be back. Finally, where there is a decision to make between leaving other children at home or spending the time at the hospital, to remember that the children at home will be in familiar surroundings, sleeping in their own beds and have around them familiar faces. The child in hospital has none of these advantages. He will be in good hands and well taken care of but with the best will in the world nurses' shifts change and there is no one person to take a parent's place during his stay.

Although this chapter has been mainly concerned with the relationship between mother and child most of what

has been said also applies to fathers, for throughout this period they have a supportive role to play. Supportive in the sense that a woman needs emotional and practical support in what is often a tiring and frustrating task. Supportive too in that a father is able to contribute to the child's growth and development in every single way that has been described here. Where this interest is present a child will benefit from the help and encouragement of both sexes. Girls, who otherwise might get involved only in bathing baby and baking cakes, will see bicycles

repaired and know the joys of football. If they bath the baby with father and repair the bicycle with mother, so much the better.

A parent–child relationship is not a good one if a child is incapable of growing through it to independence. The growth towards independence is a gradual one. The first gropings need to be gentle – not sudden and forced. When these are handled successfully other adults and friends of a child's own age will assume a greater importance in his life and he will be on the way to maturity.

Making Sense of the World

We live in a moving three-dimensional world of different shapes, colours and textures. We are surrounded by other people, some we know and love and others who are strangers. Things appear and then disappear from our sight again. As adults we can make sense of it, we understand what is going on. What does this world really look like to a young baby lying in his pram? This is the kind of question which begins practically every article I have read on the development of children, and I doubt that with all the research that has gone on in the past fifty years we have come near to finding an answer to it. Why should we be so obsessed with knowing the answer? Possibly because it is the one thing we know we must have experienced but have no knowledge of. Certainly research has shown that new-born babies can hear, that within hours of being born their eyes can follow something moving close to them, and that a sense of taste develops rapidly in the first two weeks. All the equipment is there for receiving the information we receive; but what about the equipment which makes *sense* of it all — the brain? Most of the evidence so far points to the fact that it is the inability of the brain to deal with all the information fed into the senses which makes the child's understanding of the world so different from ours. This ability to *interpret and make sense* of all that affects our senses comes only with experience and growing maturity.

There are various ways of investigating the world of young babies. One way which we can all enjoy is by very close observation of the way they react. The limitation here is that although it is quite possible to observe every move and reaction of a baby, it is hard to know whether the interpretation we place on the behaviour is the correct one. Jean Piaget, a Swiss psychologist, recorded the detailed observations made of the behaviour of his own children and thereby laid the framework we have of the way children's understanding develops.

For example, Piaget claims that children only gradually come to understand that something exists even when they cannot see it any more. Have you ever watched a baby of about five or six months playing with a rattle? He gives it his whole attention but then accidentally it falls over the edge of the pram. He appears to forget it completely and doesn't look for it at all. You pick it up and put it within his reach and he starts playing with it again. Now look at a baby a few months older in the same situation. As before the rattle falls out of the pram on to the floor. This time he certainly looks for it, first at one side, and then if it still can't be seen, on the other. He knows it is somewhere. You pick it up and he throws it out again. It becomes a game. One interpretation of this kind of incident is that somewhere in the period of about six to nine months the baby comes to realize that the rattle still exists somewhere even though he cannot see it. He has progressed from the 'out of sight out of mind' behaviour of the younger baby.

The usual explanation for this is that seeing alone cannot provide information about the existence of an invisible object. As adults we can reach for it, touch it and know that it is there. The very young baby cannot normally do this, so for him his rattle has ceased to exist. Recent research work in Edinburgh has thrown doubts on this. It provides a good example of the second type of approach to investigating the world of babies, the experimental one. In one series of experiments these researchers investigated babies of 20, 40, 80 and 100 days. In each case the baby was put to sit supported in front of an object so that he could see it. The researchers then moved a screen across, hiding the object from the baby. They reasoned that if the baby still believed that the object existed behind the screen then he would be surprised to find that this was not so. They measured this surprise by a change in heart rate. When they drew back the screen and the object was no longer there the youngest babies seemed to be surprised provided the time between the covering of the object and subsequently removing the screen was short. Only the older babies were surprised

when longer intervals were allowed to elapse. It was concluded that there is some 'built in' process which tells a baby that an object exists even when he cannot see it. This idea was confirmed for them in another experiment where they observed the babies' eye movements, and saw that the babies' eyes continued moving beyond the point where an object disappeared behind a screen to the point where they anticipated its appearance again.

These results were followed up with a very interesting experiment. By an arrangement of mirrors they were able to show a baby three images of the same person, or three images of three different people. When presented with one image of its mother and two of strangers the very young baby reacts happily with the mother and ignores the strangers. It also reacts happily to each of three images of the mother in turn. Babies older than twenty weeks also ignored the strangers and responded to the mothers but were upset at the sight of more than one 'mother' image. By now they know they have only one mother. How they come to discover this is not understood. Once it is discovered it must make the infants' world simpler. This is another example of a situation where the ability to *sort out* the information has to develop before young children are able to interpret it in the same way as adults 'see' it.

Does a young baby see everything in three dimensions as we do, or is the concept of depth something that has to be learned? There are experiments designed to test this too. The 'visual' cliff is one of them. The test is designed so that a central bridge area leads to normal floor on one side and to a 'drop' covered by a sheet of glass on the other. The baby is placed on the bridge while his mother tries to entice him to crawl over the glass covering the drop. The baby will not leave the bridge on that drop side, but he will crawl happily on the other side of the floor. So by the time a baby is crawling it does seem that he can appreciate a drop. Before you become too trusting of your baby's sense of 'drop' don't forget that *they* often forget where their legs are and swing round in such a way

that they would certainly fall into the drop if it were not covered by glass.

I have described a few of the experiments devised to explore what a baby sees and what sense he can make of it. As I mentioned earlier we cannot know exactly what he sees, but it is probable that the brain of a young baby can handle only a fraction of the information that comes in through his senses. It is the interpretation of information which develops step by step as he grows older.

Piaget divides this development of children's understanding into four main stages: from birth to about eighteen months (all the activities of babies described so far fall into this period), from about eighteen months to six or seven years, from about six or seven to about eleven or twelve, and from twelve or thirteen upwards. The exact ages at which the different stages are reached are not important and Piaget stresses this, but the order in which the stages are passed through does not change.

To develop the first stage of understanding, a young child needs the experience of seeing objects of all colours, shapes and sizes, of hearing different sounds and of feeling different textures, before he can begin to make sense of them. Since as a very young baby he is not able to seek these things for himself, it is up to the adults around him to make sure he does not live in an isolated void. There is a great deal of evidence that children, brought up in situations where they are deprived of the individual attention and affection which provide these experiences, can become retarded in their development. Playing with a baby, speaking to him, making sure he has something to look at and handle, even changing his nappy, are all situations in which he can be given the opportunity to learn about the world around him.

When a child is able to crawl and finally walk, what he sees and understands of the world progresses rapidly. He can now go after things which attract his attention, pick them up, feel them, suck them, turn them around and examine them from all sides. In this way he learns a great deal about them. Some things give to the touch, and others are hard, some things are small and can be put inside others, some things have holes in them and fit on to a finger, some things tear, others are tough. All these things we now take for granted, we once had to learn.

All this is taking place in the present. The child operates in the 'here and now'. So far he has no language – no symbols for the past or future. Over eighteen months, when real language develops, as distinct from just repeating words, a child starts playing games of make believe. He is also entering Piaget's second stage. This gives us the clue that he is now able to re-create scenes and actions in his mind and can use symbols to represent those thoughts. Catherine feeding her Teddy from her toy tea-set is re-creating the family meal times in her play.

Once a child is able to speak to us the quality of his understanding is easier to investigate. However, because language develops slowly and does not immediately take the place of action, his thinking remains very much tied to his actions and the way he sees things with his eyes dominates the way he interprets them.

Imagine a group of children at a birthday party. They are all about three to four years old. An argument develops over who has the most orange juice. Nigel has his in a tall thin glass. Caroline's is in a short fat one. In an attempt to prove to Caroline that Nigel has no more than his share you pour hers into a tall thin glass too. Not a drop is spilt, but if you now ask Caroline whether there was more orange juice in the first glass or the second, she may tell you the second, or she may tell you the first. It is unlikely that she will tell you that it is the same. To you it is self-evident that pouring the juice from one container to another does

not change the amount. It does not appear like this to a child at Caroline's stage of development.

Those children who are prepared to give you explanations about why there is more to drink in the tall thin glass claim 'it's much more bigger' or 'because it's much more thinner' or 'because you poured a lot more' (you certainly did not) or 'because I have eyes'. Some choose the wider glass as having more – 'it's fatter'. Now try it with some older children. Matthew at five and a half says of the tall thin glass 'it's much more thinner so it can go higher'. You detect a glimmer of reason and proceed

further. You start again with two empty glasses of the same shape and size and ask him to pour the orange juice into the two glasses so that there is the same amount for each of you to drink. He does so carefully and accurately until he's satisfied. This is how the conversation went when we did this:

'So if you were to drink all of this and I were to drink all of that we'd have the same amount to drink?'

'Yes.'

'All right now, I'm going to pour mine into here (a wider, shorter glass). Now if I drink all of this orange juice and you drink all of that, will we have about the same amount to drink, or will one of us have more?'

'Not really.'

'Why not?'

'Mine's higher than yours.'

'But didn't you tell me that this one is fatter?'

'Yes.'

'So what happens to the orange juice?'
'Er. It's spreaded out a bit more.'
'So do we have the same amount to drink?'

'No, not really.'

He seems to be teetering on the edge of seeing it our way but then opts for the evidence of his eyes only because the orange juice is higher in the glass.

It's no use pretending that this experiment explains exactly how the child thinks, but it certainly tells us he doesn't think in the way we do. Piaget describes a child's thinking at this stage as being concrete. The child is not just thinking like an immature adult, but in a different way from an adult.

When Piaget's work was first described in America, one of the first reactions was 'how can we speed up a child's progress through the stages?' One interesting experiment set out to find the effect that 'coaching' had on speeding up understanding. The experimenter investigated the children's reaction to whether they thought that changing the shape of a ball of plasticine also

changed its quantity. First of all he showed them the plasticine as a ball, then rolled it into a sausage. As in the orange-juice experiment, the younger children thought there was 'more' plasticine in the sausage. Some of the children were then taken and deliberately 'taught' the idea that there was the same amount of plasticine in both cases. This they did by weighing the plasticine both as a ball and in its sausage shape. Then they repeated the first investigation again. This time the investigator took away a little of the plasticine, without the children seeing, before rolling it into a sausage. When it was then weighed it of course weighed less than when in its original ball shape. The children who had been 'coached', stood by what they had been taught and maintained that the amount of plasticine had not changed. The older children who had really understood the idea, that changing the shape alone does not change the quantity, were immediately suspicious and suggested that somehow some plasticine had been lost or taken away. It does seem that in this case training did not promote true understanding of something for which the children were not ready. It was least effective where the children were much younger than the age at which the understanding usually develops. This doesn't mean, however, that the practice and experience do not help a concept develop in its own time.

A child round about the age of four is influenced by two things when faced with a problem: (a) what he sees — the orange-juice experiment shows how this dominates his way of approaching a problem — and (b) his point of view. He seems to be unconscious of the fact that there is a different point of view to his. He appears to find it hard to put himself in another position. When, for instance, he tries to explain to you how something works or recounts an incident of which you have no previous knowledge, he seems to make very little allowance for your position in the way he uses his words to explain. It is also true, of course, that in explaining to children, we as adults are often equally guilty of this. But in our case it is more likely to be thoughtlessness than a lack of understanding.

Although Piaget did not carry out his research with practical applications in mind, his results and conclusions have had an enormous influence on our ideas of the way

children learn. The water play and sand tray of nursery schools are based on the understanding of the young child's need to handle materials, to pour them from one container into another, to feel them before he can understand them. A child who fills a bottle with water, then pours half away, and then again pours away one half of that, is better prepared to understand the meaning of half, quarter and so on than by being introduced to them as rather obscure figures on a board or a page. It may seem hard to believe, but the fact that a half of a half really is a quarter only came to me clearly in a flash one day in my early twenties. I was attending a teachers' course on primary mathematics. We were all playing with the simple apparatus children used in a classroom. I followed the instructions on the card. Fill the bottle with water. Now pour half of it away. Now pour half of this away. Left as I was with a bottle quarter full of water, the $\frac{1}{2}$ of $\frac{1}{2} = \frac{1}{4}$ at last took on a real meaning and I 'understood' for the first time. Children lucky enough to be in our good primary schools today will be under no such misconceptions at my late age. What is the point of learning a symbol for a quarter until you know what a quarter is? By handling things, feeling their shape, size, texture and weight, children are 'learning' about them. They are not just 'playing'. Of course they don't go on doing this indefinitely; there is no point in hoping they will discover all the secrets of the universe themselves – they obviously want a good teacher who knows where to lead and how to follow up a child's interest.

So, although it is not possible nor desirable to force a child from one stage of thinking to another, it is necessary to make sure that he has a wide range of experiences which will lead him to a better understanding at each stage of his development.

Let us look at some concrete examples of this understanding through experience. At eighteen months
Catherine and Nick are at the toddling stage, and can get
anywhere in the house by one means or another and
choose for themselves what they want to explore. It may
be a saucepan, a lid and a mop; or it may be one of their
special toys. They learn from both of them; fitting a
round lid into a round hole (the saucepan) Nick is matching
shapes. Poking the mop into the saucepan he is physically experiencing inside, outside. Putting the saucepan
on his head he is carrying out the meaning of 'upside
down'. This way he will come to understand the relationship things have to one another. Children don't need
expensive toys for this, though many are designed for the
purpose. The coloured post office box with five different
shapes for posting is also a way of learning to match
shapes (but a more expensive one). Easiest to get in is the

circle, then the square – Catherine has a bit more trouble with the triangle and considerable difficulty with the star. When she fails to 'post' the shape she struggles until she

hears it drop into the box, muttering away to herself at the same time as trying to force it in. It seems to be something she must do. Sometimes in desperation she hands it to her mother – with a look which says 'I can't get it in so you try.' When she hears it drop she laughs with happiness and relief. The circle of events which began with picking up the shape has ended with the shape falling through the hole into the box – as she has come to expect.

Children learn from their play and we can learn a great deal about their learning from watching them carefully. For instance, although children can perceive colours, in a normal everyday situation they may pay comparatively little attention to them. I tried this out with Nigel – he's three – in a game of coloured dominoes. Nigel plays dominoes quite well with his father and older brother. But does he put the six with the six because of the shape of the dots, or because they are both the same colour? I drew a pattern of six dots in black on a piece of paper and asked him to hand me a domino which matched – he did so easily. I did the same thing with a three – instant success. Then I drew the pattern of five dots. At first he handed me a four. I then drew four dots and asked him to give me the matching domino. He looked long and hard and said: 'I just did.' So Nigel used mainly his recognition of shapes to play this game and not colours.

We are also told that children can recognize shapes before they can copy them. Nigel was still cooperative so I tried this out. First I drew a circle. Nigel easily copied this, even if he had difficulty in making the beginning and end of his circle meet. Copying my triangle proved a problem. He knew it had a bottom and put that in, then he drew in the sides. They didn't meet at the top and even as he drew it and looked at it he could see there was something wrong, but putting it right defeated him. Angles are obviously difficult for a child of this age. Indeed on one occasion Nigel copied my triangle as a circle and then just marked in the angles with lines. When I tried this with Catherine at three and a half she said: 'I can't draw the star at the top of the triangle – you draw it.' (She was pointing at the top of the triangle.) I drew it for her again very slowly. She concentrated hard as she tried to copy it, but eventually gave up and left the triangle open. Recognizing and reproducing the relation-

ships of one thing to another also develops in stages.
Inside and outside comes fairly early. I drew a circle and
then another inside it – Nigel copied this easily. I then
asked him to draw me. My arms and ears both grew out
of my head and I had no body between my head and my
legs. It isn't that he saw me like this, but like other
children of his age he found it difficult to re-create the
relationship of the different parts in his drawing. Matthew, who is two years older than Nigel, did a drawing of
me, and got these relationships correct, but he gave my
hand only three fingers. I asked him if that was all he
thought I had. 'No,' he said, 'you've got five but three's
more easier to draw.'

Within their limit of ability children tend to draw in
everything they know about an object. For instance Colin

(five) drew me a car — it had four wheels in a row along one side. I asked him why he had drawn four when I could only see two — his answer: ''cos it's got four wheels.' John drew a caravan, and although it was an outside drawing of a caravan he had also put in everything that was inside. There was a wall to the caravan, but through it we could see all the furniture — again ''cos it's there.' Eventually, partly due to an improvement in dexterity, partly to an unconscious copying of adult conventions, and partly because of their development in understanding, children's drawings take on more recognizable shape and form with attempts at perspective and profile. At first they rarely attempt any profile drawings of people although they often draw animals this way. A person or doll drawn from the side will show the two eyes and ears of a front view. Their drawings at any stage are not 'wrong', they encompass a child's limits of understanding of symbols — shapes and relationships at any given stage; and even more important, they express what he wants to express at the time. The best contribution we as adults can make is to provide children of this age with paint, paper and somewhere to paint where it doesn't matter if they make a mess.

At the end of our drawing session Nigel said: 'I'll draw you something.' He started with a good rectangle and carefully drew four small circles inside it. The fact that I didn't recognize it had more to do with my lack of imagination at that moment than the quality of the drawing. It was something he could draw — the basic shape was a square, the only other shape was a circle which he could also cope with, and the relationship of one to the other was outside/inside. He had used up all he could cope with at his age and produced me the television set I was sitting next to (the circles were the knobs).

60

When Catherine finished drawing she said 'now you draw a tree'. It seemed fair enough after all my requests of her. I drew a tree with some apprehension – she had been rather critical of a house I drew earlier. When I finished my tree she said 'I think that's a beautiful tree', and I felt the glow which comes from this kind of appreciation.

This recognition and reproduction of shapes is of course important in reading and writing. It takes very accurate recognition of shape to be able to distinguish, say, a 'b' from a 'p'. At first young children do not appear to pay much attention to the direction of shapes. They make no particular distinction between left and right and

consequently easily confuse, for example, the letters like 'b' and 'd', or draw their 'c' the wrong way round. Children of five may be unable to see the difference between a shape and its mirror image even if this is pointed out to them. Similarly they often fail to distinguish an 'n' and 'u' where one looks like the other upside down. Most of them eventually learn to do this without any difficulty. A few do not and the reasons for this are not entirely understood. What is recognized is that the ability to read and write is not just a matter of recognizing and reproducing shapes. It also involves wanting to read and having something to write about. This is why the treatment of slow readers is such a controversial and complicated subject, with many different solutions depending on the particular problem of the child. And what is true of reading and writing in relation to a child's understanding of shapes is also true of the development of his understanding generally. There are isolated areas which can be investigated and interpreted, but the way in which the understanding of any child develops is a mixture of his own particular experiences and of the relationships he has with his 'teachers' at home and at school.

Our responsibility as adults is to introduce children to the situations in which they can learn, and to give the right kind of help when asked. This does not mean solving every problem for them nor pushing them into things which interest us. A child learns at his own pace – trying to force him forward more often than not has the opposite effect. He needs to develop his own interests and to explore them in his own time. If we are genuinely interested we will find out what these interests are and make it possible for them to be developed. This way the understanding at each stage will become firmly based and something which he can build on to take the next step.

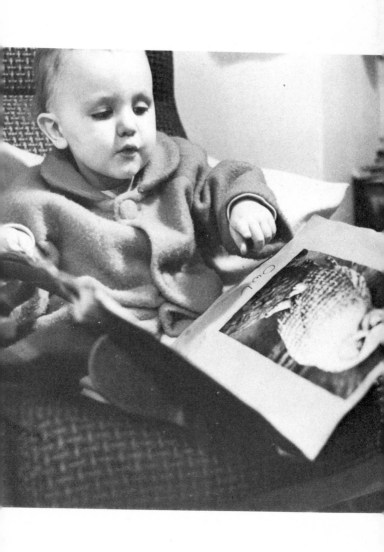

The Growing Body

Getting bigger is the one visible sign of children growing up that we can all follow, and interest in it starts very early on, so that 'how heavy?' is one of the first questions asked of every new parent. The greater the weight, the more pride there is in the answer. Young children feel like this about size too. I once produced a television programme for schools where we asked the children to send in their weight at birth. I was flooded with claims of the 20 lb. variety! Throughout the first few months this preoccupation with size persists. Many of the mothers I have spoken to at child welfare clinics go there mainly to get the baby weighed — however, the doctors and nurses in attendance see it as a very small part of their job. Gain in size is of course one indication of development; but it is by no means the most important. It is the way the nerves, muscles and bones of the body are developing, each to their own pattern, but working in harmony together, which is the fundamental part of growth. The way children are able to control the different parts of the body at any one time depends on how well harmonized these different parts are.

One of the things to look out for is the way the proportions of the body change with age. Where children span the age group from babyhood to five in any one family this change in body proportion is easy to see.

The Nash family, Eloise (six months), Guy (two), Thomas (four) and Romy (five and a half) illustrate the growth pattern at different ages. At six months Eloise's head is large compared with the rest of her body. It is much nearer its adult size than her limbs. Her brain is already about half of its adult weight. Contrast this with her whole body weight, which is less than a tenth of what she will finally be as an adult. Guy at two is now growing at a much slower rate. With his relatively short plump legs (they are no longer than his body) he is still an enlarged baby shape. By four, Thomas's age, the proportions have changed – his legs are much longer, his head smaller in relation to the size of his body. His face does

not have the chubby baby look of Guy's. The longer leg length is even more noticeable in Romy, and now at five and a half her body has reached about half of its final size, and her brain nine-tenths of its maximum size.

For an accurate assessment of the body's maturity doctors look at the developing bones, usually those of the hand and wrist. This is an area where a large number of

ELOISE

separate bones grow. It can also be easily X-rayed
without radiation reaching the rest of the body. In a new-
born baby there are no true bones in the wrist – the
structures which will later become bones are soft and
gristly and do not register on an X-ray. By examining
many children, standard guides of skeletal age in the
wrist region have been produced. By comparing the

X-rays of any child with the standard guides doctors can tell what state of physical maturity a child has reached. Some interesting information has emerged on sex differences. Girls are on average four weeks ahead of boys in skeletal age at birth and the boys remain at about 80 per cent of the skeletal maturity of girls of the same age until their teens.

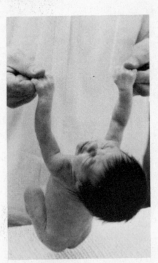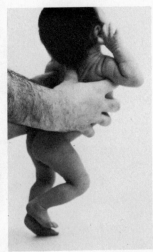

The fundamental changes by which a child develops from a helpless crying baby to a sturdy, mobile, chatty toddler take place in harmony and although the actual time at which a given child sits up, crawls, walks and runs may differ from others, the order in which these landmarks occur stays the same. Each stage is reached in its own time when the brain, nerves, bones and muscles are all ready, so it is not possible, nor even desirable, to try and force a child from one stage to another. Many people who totally accept this idea in relation to walking seem to forget it when it comes to toilet training. A child can no more control his bladder and bowels before his body is ready for it than he can reason before his brain is ready for that.

Let us look now at the way in which these changes influence the way a baby behaves. A new-born baby like Jason has little control over his movements but doctors can tell if the reactions of the nervous system are opera-

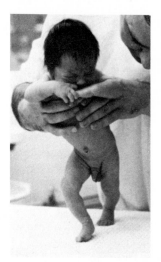 

ting correctly by stimulating certain basic reactions over which the baby has no control – his reflexes. A healthy, new-born baby has a grasp reflex. He closes his fingers around anything placed in his hand. It is such a strong grip that it can support his whole weight. (Although doctors use this as a test it is not advisable to try it out on a baby yourself. Just let him grip your finger instead, and you will still feel the strength of his grasp reflex.)

For the first six weeks or so a baby can 'walk'. The doctor holds the baby up and leans him forward – the normal baby responds then by stepping forward and 'walking' along the table. Then there is the 'startle' reflex, present for about three or four months. To produce this the doctor allows the baby's head to drop. The baby throws out his hands and then brings them together over his body. These are some of the reflexes doctors use in their examinations and should not be tried at home. But there are reflexes which you can easily see for yourself. When you touch a baby's face near his mouth he moves his mouth towards your finger. It is this 'rooting' reflex which enables a baby to find the nipple at the breast. Mothers feeding their babies soon discover that stroking a baby's foot stimulates the 'sucking' reflex.

All these reflexes eventually disappear and are gradually replaced by movements which the baby can control, and these in turn show us how well the baby is developing. For instance you can observe the changing sequence of events as a baby's ability to reach out and grasp develops, simply by seeing what happens when you put a ball or a child's brick in front of him.

A three-month-old baby can control his eyes but however hard he tries he can't reach out for a ball with his hand. And he does try hard. He huffs and puffs and dribbles and puts all he has into it, but without success. It looks very frustrating to an adult, but there is no way of knowing what it feels like to a baby. However, in a few months his arms and hands are free and also under his control. At first the hand is not a very refined piece of equipment – it acts all in one piece like a shovel. The baby covers the ball completely with the palm of his hand in order to pick it up. When he succeeds at this stage he usually puts it straight into his mouth. If you give him a second thing to hold he will often drop the first. Later he can hold two things together, one in each hand. He will often bang them together in front of his face on a table. Then comes an absolutely crucial step. When a baby uses his thumb and forefinger together to pick something up he is in a sense re-creating an evolutionary landmark. It is this ability which man has, to control the thumb and forefinger together, that separates his power of manipulation

from those of the rest of the animal kingdom. So when your baby reaches out and picks up a smartie in this way you can now view his achievement in a new light. With this development the hand can perform the most intricate tasks. Remember that even a simple action like using a spoon to eat can come only as a result of months of practice in picking things up. It is an inevitable sequence of events which has to be gone through a step at a time. Each stage follows on from the last as the child gradually moves towards feeding himself. Practice in each new-

found skill as it appears helps a child to become skilful with his hands. Many toys are designed to do this. Building towers of bricks, threading plastic balls on sticks, pushing differently shaped objects through holes all help, though expensive toys are not essential − saucepans, spoons, cotton reels all give a child practice in handling and manipulating things.

There is a similar sequence of events in a child learning to walk. First of all the walking reflex described above disappears. Then over a period of months the muscles,

bones and nerves develop together until by about six months the legs are strong enough to bear most of a child's weight. When he is ready a child will usually pull himself up to a standing position on his own initiative using a side of a playpen or a piece of furniture. This progresses through walking around the furniture, walking with a little support from a helping hand, to taking his first staggering steps alone.

It is the timing of the development of all the different parts of the body so that it works as one completely harmonized whole which is so amazing. By the time a child's legs and body are well enough developed for him to crawl around and reach something which takes his fancy, his arms, hands and fingers and eyes have also developed to the stage which allows him to reach out, pick it up and explore its possibilities. Together they make this part of his life the age of exploration. Between birth and two most of the interesting physical landmarks are reached and by the age of two growth has slowed down noticeably so that from two to five the interesting developments are in the way the child's actions and movements become more coordinated and refined. You can see this developing by watching children of different ages playing ball. A simple thing like catching a ball is a very complicated task for a three-year-old. He has to judge and compute speed, distance, size and flight path and then make sure his hands are in the right place at the right time. It's too much for Catherine, who is three and a half years old. She screws up her eyes, often closing them altogether, sticks out her hands about a foot apart and 'plonk' the ball drops through them.

The waiting-room of any child welfare clinic is full of children at all the different stages in their growth and development. As we have seen, there are great variations in size and ability, even in children of the same age. Doctors like to see children at certain specific ages when it is easier to assess their progress. This applies particularly to the six weeks, six months and ten months visits: the reason is that shortly before these times important transition stages should have occurred. The visits at eighteen months, two years, three years and four years are also influenced by this fact and by the need for immunization at certain times. The way a child responds to his mother and the doctor, plays with bricks put in front of him (or for older children, other toys in the room) and reacts to vision and hearing tests all provide the doctor with information which he can compare against standard guides of assessments. A large one-year-old may be taller

and bigger than a small two-year-old but obviously not as much can be expected of his coordination, speech and general understanding. From the observation of thousands of children, standard guides to development have been drawn up. Using them a doctor can assess how the development of any child compares with the average and if development in every aspect is occurring normally.

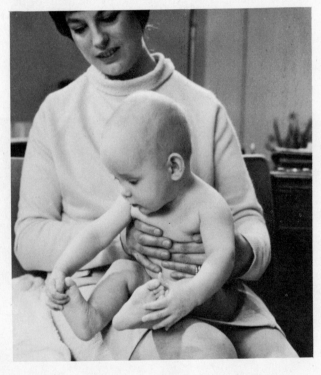

The first child to see the doctor the afternoon I was there was David. He is a very jolly five-and-a-half-months old, and he is happy enough to sit stripped on his mother's knee. He smiles and chuckles at the doctor and indeed at anyone else who pays him some attention. His main occupation in life at the moment is playing with his toes. He is more interested in these than the bricks placed in front of him, though he does finally lunge out at the bricks and picks one up. While David's attention is occupied the doctor creeps behind him and gently rings a small bell. David pauses and turns, chuckling again when he sees the doctor over his mother's shoulder. He has heard the bell's sound. If defects of seeing and hearing can be detected at this early stage it can save a great deal of trouble later. Next the doctor puts him to sit on a blanket, checking how well he holds himself up and how easily he is overbalanced. Finally with David lying on the blanket looking upwards he can check how well David's eyes follow the fluffy doll the doctor passes in an arc from side to side. The examination is almost over but one important thing remains – if David's mother has anything on her mind that is worrying her now is the time to mention it. Apparently she hasn't, but promises to bring him back again in three months' time.

Helena is the next child the doctor sees. She is two and a half years old. At first she does not want to leave her mother's side, and even when she is persuaded to play with the toy tea-set on the table she keeps her gloves on – she doesn't intend to stay and this is her way of saying so. She is eventually persuaded to take them off, and goes to play with the cups and saucers. The doctor watches to see how skilfully she manipulates them and how well she understands their use. A child who plays at pouring tea from the pot into the cup and then gives the doll a drink has a good understanding of the way these things are done in the real world outside her playthings. After he has watched her playing for a while he finds out how well she sees and speaks. As he points to each picture she names it. This again tells him how well she understands. To recognize a picture of a cup and to call it a cup may not seem much to an adult, but it is an achievement for a two-and-a-half-year old. Next Helena helps the doctor

build a tower of bricks. First he puts on a brick, then Helena puts one on top of it. Now it's the doctor's turn again and so on. The higher the tower gets the harder it is to balance the bricks and the doctor can observe the limits of Helena's coordination and manipulation. Finally he moves to the other end of the room from Helena and picks up a box of small toys. In turn he holds up a toy car, a tiny fork, a spoon and a knife. Each time he asks Helena to call out what she sees. This she does quietly and shyly, but accurately. This way he is testing her distant vision and again her understanding.

This examination is not a test to grade children: it is a way of identifying possible defects which if they are recognized early enough can be prevented from handicapping a child throughout its life. Without such tests perfectly normal and intelligent children who are just not hearing properly may be thought slow and retarded, and children with bad eyesight may never make out the jumbled shapes on the blackboard and printed page.

At the age of five a child is usually ready to start school. The Plowden Report on primary education recommends a complete examination before a child enters school because a school day can be very demanding. He has to learn to get on with new adults and other children, to share the games and toys which are around, and to take turns at the things he likes doing best. The day itself begins at 9 a.m. with assembly and ends six to seven hours later. This can be physically and psychologically demanding for a young child. An examination at four and a half could alert teachers and parents to possible problems. A child who attends a pre-school playgroup or nursery school can be introduced to this new world more slowly, and can adjust to it at his own pace.

To sum up, all the skills and abilities which emerge as a child grows up do so in a certain order and at their own rate. No amount of forcing can develop them earlier. Parents can play their part in the process by making sure that the child has the practice and encouragement he needs to fulfil his potential one step at a time.

Learning to Speak

Have you ever been in a country and not been able to speak the language? The stages you pass through in trying to achieve some sort of contact with the natives probably go something like this. First of all you point and mime your needs with humorous, if not always successful, results. Then you pick up the essential everyday nouns, water, butter, coffee. Soon you're ready to chance your arm at two words at a time — some learnt parrot-fashion from listening to others — 'good morning'; 'how are you?'; 'good-bye' — others a combination of one well practised adjective used with a number of different words — *cold* orangeade or *cold* beer, and so on. It's a while before you take a chance on verbs, and then you're quite likely to end up with the 'me go', 'no want' variety. Fluency in the language can take years and much sweat and toil, and the native accent may never be achieved.

Superficially a child learning to speak a language passes through stages just like this. But inside far more interesting things are taking place. As a stranger in a foreign land, you at least know what language is — that it is made up of words which stand for things around us, actions, past, present and future. A baby is not born knowing this. It is not until the end of his first year that he begins to show that he realizes words stand as symbols for things. The process leading up to this stage and beyond it into sentences is a fascinating period in the development of any child. It is the period when we can see and hear the one thing developing which makes human beings unique – a language.

Learning to speak is a complicated process. It involves first of all the development of a general understanding of the world we live in, a facility for making the right sounds correctly and clearly, and finally putting together these sounds into words and sentences which express our thoughts in a way others can understand. These three things are, of course, going on simultaneously. And their development in any child involves a great deal of conscious and unconscious teaching on somebody's part. This teaching begins in earliest childhood. We can see it in the most ordinary everyday scenes. Bathing, for instance.

This baby is six weeks old. Although a baby of this age is far from talking, this bath scene is certainly not taking place in silence:

'Who's a lucky girl then?' (coos from baby). 'Come on' (gurgles). 'There's a good girl, aren't you, eh?' (gurgles).

'I know you don't like your face wiped. Lift your chin up, lift your chin, that's it.' (All this punctuated by sounds of annoyance from the baby.) 'Hello' (gurgles). 'Yes, you've got a lot to say, haven't you? Come on, have your neck washed. There you are, there's a good girl, aren't you, eh? I know you don't like it. There you are – there's some lovely milk in there.'

Her mother is smiling and the sound of her voice is warm and gentle. The baby is getting practice in hearing all the different sounds in the English language. She's not making any of her own yet, but it's important that she hears them all the same. At the same time she is learning to distinguish the different tones of her mother's voice.

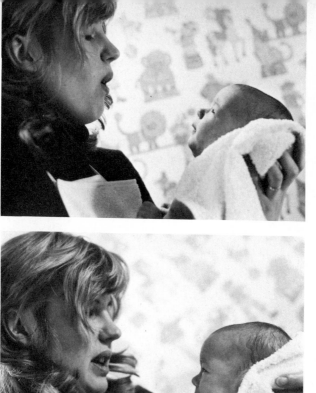

She can associate these tones with the expression on her mother's face, and eventually with the movements of her lips.

Fortunately there is something about a baby which makes most adults want to carry on this kind of conversation, but sometimes it doesn't happen – a mother may feel no interest in her child – the nappy changing becomes mechanical – and her mind and interest are elsewhere. Carry this feeling over into bathing, feeding

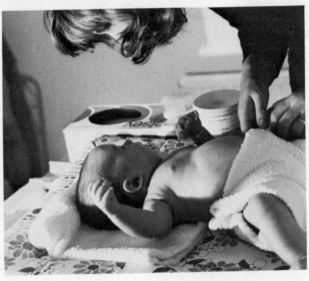

and bedtime, and where would a baby ever get to hear the different noises and sounds of the language? Where would he experience the closeness of a relationship in which he learns to communicate? For it is in these everyday situations that the foundations are laid for learning to speak. If a child does not receive this individual coaching in the first four years, and most particularly the first two years of life, he will have great difficulties in learning to speak.

How does a child convey to us that he is beginning to understand? And how can we help this understanding to develop? Catherine is a fairly typical one-year-old. The details of what and how she learns will vary in another child, but the general pattern is the same for all. For months now every time her mother dresses her she has heard 'sleeves out', 'arms in', 'slippers off', 'feet in'. Every

action and every thing has a word that stands for it. This is what she is unconsciously learning and being taught. Hearing them repeated in these familiar contexts every day helps her recognize them and respond to them long before she can use them herself. This understanding, that words can stand as a code for action and things, comes gradually and would not come at all to a child who was not hearing language. This is another reason why it is so important to speak to children at this stage, although they cannot speak to us.

By eighteen months Catherine shows that she understands more complicated sentences. Her mother is ironing and Catherine is playing in a corner of the room. Periodically she comes for attention – help in blowing up a balloon, taking off a lid that has jammed. She isn't asking for help with words, but with appealing sounds and gestures. Her mother is anxious to get on with the ironing and says 'Go and fetch Teddy to play with, Catherine', and off Catherine goes to the other room to fetch him. She at least understands the word 'teddy' and probably 'go and fetch'. Rather unsteadily she heaves him back, and puts him in a chair, head downwards, legs in the air. Mother says: 'Oh Catherine, you've put him on his head – he's upside down. I'm sure he'll be more comfortable if you turn him round.'

Catherine looks hard at Teddy for a few seconds and puts him the right way up. It seems as though she understands what it means to be 'upside down' and to 'turn him round'. She shows us this by her actions. She is storing up these words and experiences and may not use them until much later. The first time I heard Catherine use 'upside down' was six months later. She was playing with animals in a toy farm and stood a squirrel on its head.

'Mummy, it's (hesitantly) upside – upside down.' Her mother says – 'Yes, that's right, it's upside down.'

Catherine looked very pleased with herself at this. She had used the phrase correctly for the first time, but it had been there for at least six months. I wonder if it's the same kind of pleasure and relief of achievement I feel at actually being handed what I've asked for in a shop in Italy or Spain.

If we watch children using their toys and playthings they give us many clues to how well they are beginning to understand the world around them. They don't need expensive toys. Old saucepans, spoons, cups, brushes, dish mops – all provide a child with different shapes,

surfaces, colours and textures. At twenty-one months Catherine enjoys playing with tiny cups and saucers, and miniature replicas of everyday things like combs and brushes. Her play is now entering a world of make-believe, an important landmark in development. Surrounding her are Teddy, Dolly and Seabag (a huge

Gonk). She feeds Teddy and Seabag from the tiny cups. Next she turns her attention to their hair, brushing it vigorously. When it's finished she gives Teddy a look at himself in the mirror. Teddy's feet are also hairy – they can be brushed, so she brushes those with a hair brush too. She shows up how well she understands the way these objects are used. She has seen her mother and father drinking from a big cup, and can make her tiny cups stand for 'cup' and 'drinking' as they do in the everyday world outside her toys' world. She doesn't need water – this is a world of make-believe. When she uses the hair brush on her own hair, her doll's and Teddy's, she uses it as she has seen it used. Organizing her toys like this is only one stage before organizing her words about them. She's nearly ready now to use words as she's heard them used. That is why it is so important that children get a chance to play like this – it allows them to develop their understanding of the way things are. At twenty-one months Catherine is at the stage of 'naming' everything. She has understood for some months that everything has a name – now she really wants to know what the name is. A trip to the zoo full of things new to her is a field-day of naming. She stops in front of the monkey's cage –

Catherine: 'Mo-mo-monkey.'

Mother: 'That's right – it's a monkey. Here he comes, isn't he a lovely monkey?'

Catherine: 'Monkey down.'

Mother: 'He can't get down – he's in a cage. Look, now he's scratching.'

Now a pigeon lands at Catherine's feet: shouts of glee, stamping of feet, and –

Catherine: 'Pig-pidg- . . .'

Mother: 'Yes, it's a pigeon. Give some food to the pigeon. Hold it down there.'

If we listen to the conversation we see how her mother is giving her more than the name each time – she is adding new words and ideas to it. You can overhear conversations of this kind between a mother and her child in any variety of circumstances and accents. It's as though the great pleasure of learning in the child and this unconscious teaching of the mother develop together, one feeding the other. An adult who had said 'Yes, dear, very nice', may not think she is ignoring the child, but she's not being much help to her either. She is not adding anything to the child's use of the word or giving her any idea of how to use it in a sentence. This is vital, for although individual words are of course tremendously important, we rarely use them alone.

It is in conversations and experiences like this that children come to understand that there are words that you put with other words – that you can have small monkeys, baby monkeys, furry monkeys and so on.

Catherine's first general-purpose word for putting with others was 'too'. So we got 'horsey too', 'aunty too', 'monkey', then at the sight of another one, 'monkey too'. She sometimes used it to mean 'another' but not always – it was just a word she tried out with all the other words she knew. 'Bye-bye' was her next general word. She used it first waving good-bye to her father when he went to work. Soon it was 'bye-bye' to everything as she went past it. 'Bye-bye horsey – bye-bye sheep.'

So far Catherine has not used many verbs in her speech. She has been learning them along with all the other types of words. Her first was 'look' – she made a game of it – 'lo-loo-loo-loo-look' – pointing at everything that caught her eye and she didn't want her mother to miss – then 'Mummy, what is that?'

When this sentence was discovered – first of all by repetition – grown-ups asked it of her so often – she

really worked it to death. The curiosity of the two-year-old leads to this question a hundred times a day. Over this year between one and two, Catherine has moved from mimes and gestures, through single words, combinations of words, and finally to simple sentences. For her language to be rich and varied, and her understanding to grow, she, like all children, needed a patient adult to speak to her, play with her and help her along.

So far we have looked at the development of a child's *general understanding* without which language cannot develop. But a language which nobody understands because the sounds are all wrong is of little use to anyone. Language is for communication.

Most children have their own way of making sounds at first; only as they grow older do they become more adult like us in their pronunciation. At a very early age babies normally exercise the parts of their mouths they will later use for speaking. When a baby sucks and licks his toys he is finding out about what his tongue and mouth can do, as well as what his toys feel like. At this stage his mouth is as important in his exploration as his hands. After a few months he begins to explore the possibilities of making sounds of different pitch and volume – growls, mutters, gurgles and shrieks.

Nick is eight months old. He sits on the floor in the middle of his toys and practises his sounds like a prima donna. As he leads up to his highest 'eeeee' he braces his body, raises his eyes to heaven and hits his note hard and clear. It really does look as though he is practising each new sound as he finds it.

When Nick's mother joins him in the room his sound-making stops. Now he turns his attention to the duck his mother has brought.

Mother: 'Nick, here's Mr Duck – you saw him in Kew

– do you remember – we saw him? We took the bread.'
(Nick laughs) 'Yes, you remember don't you? Here he is
– quack, quack.'

(Nick's contribution to this is gurgles and coos and the
occasional 'caa caa'.)

He seems to be imitating the sound his mother made.
Adults certainly encourage babies to imitate. A baby who
babbles 'ma ma ma – da da da' has them repeated back to
him with much approval and delight. Little wonder he
says them again and again. But apart from this a baby
will often lie alone in his cot running through a whole
string of sounds, and when he is a little older words
which he has heard earlier in the day.

Those who study children's language are divided on
the importance of this babbling stage. Some regard it as
crucial to the development of spoken language – others
that language develops independently of this stage. What-
ever the answer, eventually one or two recognizable words
appear. They are usually names of familiar things within a
child's vision and grasp which he can point at. They are the
first clear landmark of a process that has been going on
for many months – the development of a spoken language.

It's a long way from saying one word to making even
the simplest sentence. Catherine's first sentences were
repetitions of her mother's. It happens as Catherine and
her mother are playing with a toy farm – setting out the
fences, outhouses and animals.

Mother: 'It's a sheep – put it in the farm.'

Catherine: 'Put it in the farm.' (Catherine now picks
up a small building.) 'Mummy, what is this?' (This is
Catherine's stock question at the moment.)

Mother: 'It's a shed.'

Catherine (repeats): 'A shed.' Now of her own accord
she picks up another sheep and says: 'Put it in the shed.'

She has already used her new phrase 'put it in the ...' with a new noun – 'shed'. By using her simple sentences in a variety of combinations she is practising her use of them. The development of the language involves more than repetition. Catherine is also making sentences of her own – she has now picked up a bubble-making set. Unfortunately it is a very windy day.

Catherine: 'Me catch some bubble.'

Mother: 'I'll hold the thing – you blow the bubbles.'

Catherine: 'I do, I do. Catherine can't blow.'

Mother: 'No, it's difficult, isn't it?'

Catherine: '... iff – ic – ult' (she staggers through this word).

Mother: 'Here you are – up in the air – there you go – hands up, catch the bubbles.'

Catherine: 'No more run – want a potty pee pee.'

Mother: 'Do you? Well, I'll have to do something about that.'

One American scientist has investigated the ways in which a child is taught its mother tongue. She has distinguished two techniques. In the first case the adult merely gives back to the child a correct version of what the child has said. So for instance when a child says – 'Daddy gone room', the adult might say – 'Yes, Daddy has gone out of the room.' The adult is supplying the full sentence structure which was only partly there in the child's statement. She is giving him new language. She then compared this with a situation where the adult gives a more general answer to, for example, 'Daddy gone room.' The reply might be 'Yes, he's gone to move the car.' This researcher claims to have found better language progress in children spoken to in this second way than those where the sentences were merely expanded.

Most of the American work on how children acquire the grammar of a language is based on the idea that the child who is learning to speak in sentences is really learning rules. There are many fascinating investigations of this. In one, an American psychologist showed children a rather odd-looking animal toy which she called a 'wug', a nonsense word which doesn't exist. She explained to each child that 'this is a wug', and then as she

introduced another animal 'this is another wug, so there are two ...?' leaving the gap for the child to fill. We repeated this with a number of English children between three and a half and five years old. With the exception of one five-year-old who said 'wuggles' they all said 'wugs'. This is what you would expect from a child who has an idea that the general rule for making plurals is to add an 's'. She has also investigated the making of a past tense. Here 'gling' is the nonsense word. She tells the child – 'This wug glings every day. Today he glings – yesterday he ...?' again leaving a gap for the child to answer. We tried this out too, but found only the older children in the range knew what we were after. They offered 'glinged' and 'glung'. One boy threw us by saying 'didn't gling' and this was capped only by a girl who said 'wugged'.

From the results of work like this it seems that children form in their mind some general rules of language — for example, that we generally add an 's' for a plural and an 'ed' for a past tense. We can often hear them putting these rules into operation with quaint results ... 'he teached me to do it'; 'I seed him, Mummy.' These words seem like mistakes to us because we know there are such things as irregular verbs that don't obey the general rules. But children quite sensibly just apply the rule of adding an 'ed'. One of the difficulties in investigating children's language is that we can only hear what they speak and not what they understand. Since it is generally accepted that they understand more than they speak this is a serious limitation.

Although a child learns to speak from adults he practises his talking with other children. He therefore not only needs things to talk about, but other children to talk to. Communication with other people is, after all, the end-product of learning to speak. Nursery schools and playgroups provide excellent opportunities for practising and developing language — when children have things to do and play with, which interest them, they will talk.

For example, a group of four-year-olds are playing on a tower built of blocks. It is their lorry. Some are wearing Indian head-dress, others cowboy hats. At the top of the pile of blocks sits Timothy. He's driving the make-believe lorry and providing his own sound effects:

'Brr brr bar ...'

Suddenly one of his passengers jumps down and runs away.

Timothy: 'Duncan, where are you going?'

Duncan: 'I'm going to do wee wee.'

Timothy: 'Well, hurry up and come back 'cos I'm driving' (he continues his game muttering to himself).

Now Claire, another friend, approaches tentatively and tries to climb aboard:

Timothy: 'You can't climb in, you're a woman.'

Claire retires, reluctantly accepting this devastating logic. Duncan returns and takes his place behind the leader. End of scene.

These children are happy to communicate with each other, slipping from their world of fantasy to reality, and back again with ease. Words come easily to them now and they enjoy playing with them. For instance, at a tea party mixing flour and water:

'It's a pie – a dirty pie – a dirty old pie.'

'I'm making apple pie. When you put it in the oven be careful 'cos it's hot. Mine's rolled out like a thin sausage.'

Adjectives, nouns, verbs, past tense, future – they are all there and they use them to good effect – they reason with them.

All this happens slowly and naturally over the period of four years. It seems to have happened without effort, but the fact that language has developed and that these children express themselves so freely shows a great deal of conscious and unconscious teaching on somebody's part.

What about children with special speech difficulties? Most children pass through the stages of pronouncing sounds their own way and then reach clear adult-like speech. In a few this doesn't happen. The sooner they are given expert help from a speech therapist the better. For instance, Mark, at four, finds it very difficult to pronounce his sounds correctly. Many of his consonants are very indistinct. He is a confident speaker all the same, and is happy to hold a conversation.

Speech therapist: 'How did you come here today?'
Mark: 'By aar.'
Speech therapist: 'Whose car did you come in?'
Mark: 'Daddy's tar.'
Speech therapist: 'What colour is Daddy's car?'
Mark: 'Geen – dark geen. An Ortin.'
Speech therapist: 'An Austin – that's super.'

We use our lips, tongue, teeth and jaw in intricate combinations to speak our language. Try to describe to someone how to say a simple sound like 't' and you will realize what a complicated set of movements is involved. Mark hasn't got these under control yet. The therapist has to make him aware of what his tongue can do. One of the games he likes to play is 'lick the cherry'. She puts a

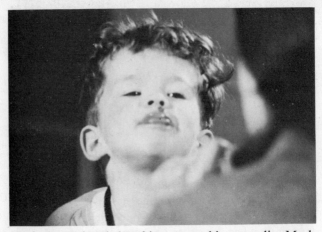

glacé cherry just below his nose on his upper lip. Mark
has to use his tongue to bring the cherry down into his
mouth. It is quite a difficult exercise – he attacks it with
gusto and is delighted with his success and the cherry
which is his reward. She also gives him the exercise of
licking a lollipop – naturally he doesn't mind this either!
The exercise is to start at the bottom of the lolly and lick
it right up to the top with long flowing movements of his
tongue. All the exercises are geared to help him get control of his tongue movements. He needs his tongue for 'l'
and 't', etc. When he says 'p' 'f' 'c' 't' correctly he should
be able to feel the air passing through his lips and teeth.
There is a game for this too. The therapist gets him to
blow a piece of cotton wool all over the table top just by
saying 'c' 'c' 'c' and 'p' 'p' 'p' very near to it. When it
moves he can see and feel the result of his efforts. Teaching him is a long process and for some time Mark will
have to think hard about the movements he needs to make
to produce the sounds correctly. This has to be achieved
without making him too self-conscious to speak at all.

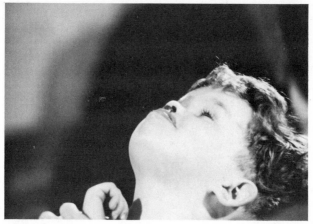

Some children are very slow in learning to talk. When faced with a silent, seemingly stubborn child it is very tempting to try and make him repeat words after you. This doesn't help. He needs to listen to groups of words in situations which have a meaning for him. It is best to put the word you want him to learn in short sentences; for example, 'reach me your shoe – put this shoe on – now the other shoe.' This way he will have heard the word a few times – each time in a different sentence.

If you are worried that your child is backward in talking, take him along to the doctor for investigation. A child who is not saying a single word at two is slow in learning to talk. If there is some special reason for the problem the sooner it is found the better. Deafness, for example, is one common cause of not talking. If children do not hear sounds and words as babies and toddlers they will not produce them later. Occasionally the reason may be a general backwardness in understanding. Tessa is a child of two who is not talking at all except for saying 'no' and a sort of 'mummy'. Doctors at the clinic have carried out tests which show she is neither deaf nor mentally backward. However, the experience of language she has had so far has not resulted in her talking and this has to be investigated. To do this the therapist plays with her and sees how good her understanding is. They are

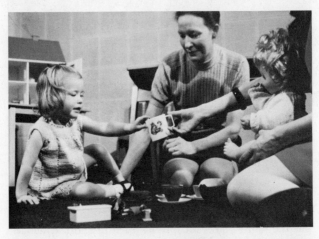

playing with some doll's-house furniture and a small doll's tea-set. The dolls form a family group. Tessa shows that she understands – 'put Mummy on the chair and give Daddy a drink' – by doing just that when she's asked to. Occasionally she ventures a sound. She is always given a chance to do this. It's vital that she at least tries, and she is rewarded with a 'well done' or some other encouragement when this happens. Tessa's mother is watching the play. The therapist explains to her what she is doing and she learns the kind of things she should do with Tessa. It's not enough that Tessa hears conversation which is not directed to her – she needs to be involved in conversations where she takes part, hears simple sentences, is asked to do things, and praised when she does. In less than a year Tessa and children like her can be helped to speak. With some children it would take longer, but in any case the earlier work begins the better. What Tessa will be getting, by way of help from the therapist in the clinic and her mother at home, is a concentrated form of the teaching through which all children naturally learn. Even more than other children she needs plenty of opportunity to listen to spoken language, to be talked to in simple sentences and told stories about herself and things she knows. For it is only through experiences like this that language develops.

The Need to Play

Play is a very misused adult word. To a child it is a way of life, but to an adult it often means the unimportant recreational things we do when we are not working. Because this is the way we think of it for ourselves, we often dismiss it in children with the remark: 'Oh, he's just playing.' But the variety and function of play in a child's life is worthy of much more serious attention than this remark implies.

So why do children play? To begin answering this question let's look at a few different examples of playing. First of all Nick. He's eight months old. For about half an hour every morning he is fastened into the baby bouncer. With the music of Radio 1 as a background he bounces and turns, squeals with delight, stops, listens and then pushes off again from the floor. Nick is playing. In this case the game is the sheer joy of moving his body around and being carried up and down by the spring of the bouncer.

Now consider the activities of Kay, Lucian and Tristan who have taken over the kitchen floor. They have a central pool of paints and are each attacking their paintings in their own way. Kay is two – he smells the paint, sloshes it around, tips some, then rubs it into the paper.

Lucian, at three and a half, dips the paint brush into the pot and concentrates hard on his picture – a mass of blue strokes. Tristan, at five, is creating a whole world of fantasy and imagination on his paper – he has recognizable houses and people. If asked what they were doing I suppose we would say 'they are *just playing* in the kitchen.'

Finally imagine a nursery school. In one corner there is a 'house' – a bank of chairs covered with curtains mark if off from the rest of the room. There are six children here ranging from three and a half to four and a half. At break, when the others are having milk and biscuits, one

of the children creeps back into the house and feeds and nurses the dolls. She is talking to herself.

'My mummy's gone away. She's gone to hospital to get a new baby. It's going to be a tiny wee one like this one. It's going to be pink. She'll come back soon, very soon. She'll come back with a new baby. A pink one.' She is working out her anxieties about the new baby, but I suppose we would also say that she is playing.

With such a wide range of examples it isn't surprising that there is no one definition of play but many, and not one single comprehensive answer to the question 'Why do children play?'

Since play is often active and boisterous one of the early functions attributed to it was the using up of surplus energy. This is certainly acceptable as a superficial reason. Recognizing this, most nursery schools and play-groups have built into their day periods of activity – dancing, marching, running etc. – to follow some previous quieter activity like building or painting and to be followed by a song or a story. However it is certainly not the whole explanation – it doesn't explain why a cross, tired toddler dragging around a shop behind his mother perks up immediately at the possibility of playing on the rocking horse outside the store.

Jean Piaget links play with the development of intelligence. He maintains that when playing a child re-creates the reality of the world around him. This goes for the material world of water, sand, bricks and mud as well

as the world of people and relationships. Play in this case is an important part of learning.

Freud links play with the emotions – and what children do in play is often closely observed and interpreted because it is believed that what they do in their play is not a chance occurrence but an expression of their feelings and emotions. For example, the little girl feeding and nursing the dolls was anxious about the fact that her mother was away and likely to return with a new baby. She was thinking about this and acting it out in her play.

I think at this stage it is best to accept that, with a word as widely used and undefined as play, there will be instances of play just for the fun of it, learning play and emotional play, all within the same game and that anyway these categories are not mutually exclusive.

As a child develops he goes through different stages of play. Very young children play alone but as they grow older they begin first of all to play with one other child and eventually are able to cooperate in a game with a larger group.

Let us look at these three stages in more detail. A baby in his pram plays alone with his toys. He sucks them, squeezes them and throws them out. If there is a willing adult to pick them up again this becomes a great game. At the crawling and toddling stage children are on the whole still solo players. Willy and Catherine are thirteen months old. Their mothers met in hospital when the children were born and have kept in contact ever since. As a result the children meet each other often, but most of their time together they spend playing alone and not with each other. Occasionally they converge on the same toy and there is a mild scuffle, but then they go their separate ways again. Catherine's interest in Willy always perks up when he is at his most vulnerable – as he lies on the carpet having his pants changed! Occasionally, too, when one of them finds something that looks interesting, like crawling upstairs, the other crawls behind and joins in the activity. But these occasions are rare and most of the time they play alone or with the adults.

By eighteen months I noticed little change in their cooperation, though their ways of playing with things had developed. Catherine is by now a great tidier and constructor, forever putting bricks into a box or piling wooden soldiers on top of an upturned bucket. Willy, on the other hand, enjoys knocking things down and does so as quickly as Catherine can arrange them. She doesn't show any sign of displeasure at this, but patiently reconstructs her arrangement. There always seem to be some children who enjoy the 'knocking down' element more than the 'building up'. Of course in many cases a child will patiently and painstakingly build a tower and then with glee knock it down himself – and will repeat this process time and time again. He is practising his new skills of picking things up, balancing them and knocking them down – and seeing them come apart. Children seem to pursue this understanding with tremendous seriousness and a sense of purpose.

Looking at children of different ages playing with each other can tell us a lot about the different stages they have reached both in their ability to get on with one another in play, and also their individual physical and intellectual development which naturally plays another large part in their behaviour. I witnessed a game of snakes and ladders

played by Kay, Lucian and Tristan. A two-year-old like Kay is not very sociable or cooperative. But Tristan (five) needs his younger brothers, in theory at least, to play against. This is how it went. Tristan had first go. He was the oldest, biggest and the boss. Then Lucian at three and a half took his turn and threw the dice — so far so good.

But, Tristan moved the counter along. Then it was Kay's turn. His movements are not yet well coordinated; he shook the dice and promptly dropped it into a large box of toys. Tristan turned the box upside down but failed to find it. With Tristan's angry shouts in his ear Kay ran screaming to his mother in the kitchen. Lucian by this time had lost interest and wandered away: and so it went on. The two-year-old, three-year-old and five-year-old do not make compatible playmates for very long, nor can we expect them to. They are at different stages of development. At five, Tristan is ready to organize and cooperate; Kay at two cannot be organized and can only be a nuisance in Tristan's eyes.

One year later Kay was much more inclined to cooperate in play. With Tristan at school, Kay (now three), and Lucian (now four and a half) and some other playmates around the same age often played together. I watched them playing garages and a hierarchy soon formed. Kay fetched and carried for Lucian, but Kay in turn ordered the girls around. This hierarchy is a changing thing. Last year Lucian had been at the bottom of the heap as he tagged along with Tristan's friends. Now he was making the most of being the elder brother while Tristan was at school. Last year when Lucian played football with Tristan's friends he was pushed, shouted at and ignored. Now with Tristan and his friends at school Lucian is the oldest boy in the game. This time it is Kay who is pushed off the ball, falls down and screams in frustration. He is a plucky three-year-old, but can't stand it for long and runs off the field.

In games like this, as well as learning to cooperate, children are developing their balance and coordination, learning to master their frustrations and to cope with relationships with other children. There were no adults around interfering with what went on. The children were sorting out the problems of their own world of play in their own way. One year ago Lucian was learning what it was like to be left out of something; now he knows what it is like to lead. Children gradually accumulate a range of experiences like this which, although they may not understand at the time, stand them in good stead when they are older.

We can also see this development from individual play to cooperative play in 'make-believe' games. A younger child of about two will 'make believe' alone. Teddy and dolly get smacked, washed, have their hair combed, are fed and put to bed. Events of the day are re-created and reconstructed. As children get older the number who can be involved in this kind of play increases. Their make-believe play copies in careful detail many scenes of adult life. They choose their roles – mummy, daddy, baby, the milkman, the baker. I watched a group of nursery school children playing like this. Duncan and Timothy were the centre of the game. They cooked and rolled out pastry. In the background the girls washed the babies and put them to bed. Eventually one of them joined the boys and lifted the 'pies' out of the 'oven'. 'Careful,' she said, 'they're hot,

very hot,' and for them those slabs of soggy dough were 'hot' pies, not to be touched for fear of burning the fingers. When children are involved in make-believe games like this they slip from fantasy to reality and back again very easily. By this age cooperative play will hold their attention for a much longer time than a year before.

Many children invent imaginary playmates. Emma, aged four, has two, Gago and Peter. Both are little boys. There was a third, Baby Boy, but he got left behind when they moved house. Gago seemed to do all the naughty things for which Emma had previously been scolded – he spilled things, crayoned on the wall, even got out of bed at night. Peter on the other hand smacks Gago when he is naughty and puts him to bed. Emma usually plays with them alone. She gives them rides on her swing and holds imaginary tea parties, but she also introduced Gago to her friend Angela and they played with him together. The invention of an imaginary playmate is very common, as you will find out if you ask your friends. It is not restricted to the only child (Emma has a sister) nor to children who are isolated from others of the same age.

Piaget maintains that make-believe play declines at about seven to eight years; as a child becomes more capable of coping with life socially and emotionally it becomes less relevant. This doesn't mean that a child stops having fantasies, but that from now on they are in thoughts and words rather than in actions. The child, thinking about people, things and actions, is now sufficiently skilled to dispense with 'props'.

We know that children imitate adults and adult behaviour in their play. They do this in a very specific way. For example when we filmed children playing, they invariably incorporated taking pictures, with toy or imaginary cameras, into their own play. (These were not necessarily the children who were being filmed, but also those playing in another part of the room.) They also imitate actions very accurately. Rosanna, a four-year-old who was washing her doll, imitated the order of events which she must have watched her mother perform many times.

Children also imitate adults in a much more general sense. This imitation is really a kind of identification; a situation in which girls model themselves on the behaviour and attitudes of their mothers and boys on those of their father. However, this general imitation is not the only way in which male children learn to be boys and female children learn to be girls. As adults we are continually making sure that they develop in these roles. When girls play at washing, bathing the baby, hanging the clothes on the line, and are gentle, we continually reinforce their behaviour by commenting favourably on it and provide the materials to develop it further. Similarly, we expect boys to be assertive, tough and mechanically minded and we reinforce this kind of behaviour in a similar way. Women's Lib begins to lose the fight right here.

How much are children otherwise influenced to the good or bad by the things they see happening around them – for example, violence? A great deal of research has been done on how and when children imitate aggression in their play. In one of these experiments a group of children watch a film where a boy of their own age behaves violently to a Bozo doll (a large rubber doll which bounces back when hit). He hits it in very specific ways – with a train or a hammer; he sits on it and punches it. After seeing the film the children were shown into a room where all these objects and many other toys were present. They were allowed to play with anything and were observed from behind a one-way mirror window. As you might expect the doll caught their attention and they started bashing it. They imitated very precisely many of the actions of the little boy they had seen on the film. They also made up many of their own. Children varied in the amount they concentrated on hitting the doll. Those who came from homes well equipped with toys and other things to play with, and were given every chance to play with them, spent less time copying the Bozo-bashing boy. They did however often hit the doll with novel methods of their own. Children deprived of toys and opportunities to play at home spent a large proportion of their time in the room hitting the doll.

So children will imitate violence and aggression in their play. However, whether or not this influences them to be aggressive and violent in the real world is not known. It is the kind of generalization that cannot be made from such experiments. The question needs answering, of course, since it is important for everyone involved in writing books or making films and television programmes for children. It also has implications for any parent – after all a parent matters to the child more than any character on the screen and is more likely to be copied. This is an important point as the kind of discipline a parent uses can affect a child's aggressive behaviour. Parents who beat their children for being aggressive think that by doing so they will stop their roughness. On the contrary – many studies have shown that aggressive parents, who use physical punishment to discipline their children, produce more aggressive children. They are, after all, making sure by doing this that the children have an aggressive model to imitate.

Watching children playing together in a house is an interesting study in group dynamics. There are dominant bosses who manipulate every aspect of the game to their own advantage; the led, who blindly follow; and, very often, the outsider who is not really accepted by the rest. Getting the outsider accepted and included in the game needs very skilful handling. Children are quick to sum up a situation and will manipulate adults for their own ends. I found this out to my cost in a nursery school. There were six children in the house, four girls and two boys. They were organizing a party. One, as it happens the largest girl, was ordering the baker and milkman around, and also doing everything she could to get rid of one of the children in the group. This child – I'll call her Lucy – was always on the fringe of the group, never part of it, though she did want to be in on the party. Seeing the bullying that was going on I joined them and tried to find out what was happening and why. I thought one solution was to make Lucy a guest at the party – this they promised to do, the leader quickly realizing that this would mean that Lucy would temporarily at least have to go outside the house and then be invited in. True, they eventually did invite her in but, in the short term, the leader had won. By incorporating my suggestion into her

plans, she pleased the adult and satisfied herself, so killing two birds with one stone. A wily move. I vowed to tread more carefully in a situation like this next time, but what would you have done?

We have to tread warily whenever we enter the young child's world of play and try to organize it. Most of their play is spontaneous and is not governed by fixed rules. The idea of rules and their adoption develops in stages — as part of their intellectual development.

Piaget has studied children's attitudes to rules, using the following technique. He joined a group of children playing marbles, and he then asked them to let him play, and because he did not know how to play, to explain the rules to him. From his studies he concluded that from about four to eight years a child sees rules as adult-given, sacred and unchangeable. From about eight onwards rules can be mutually agreed with one's friends.

Seeing rules as sacred and unchangeable doesn't mean that a young child under five will naturally obey them to the letter. On the contrary, his self-centred approach often makes him bend the rules to his own advantage. We

watched a group of four-year-olds playing picture dominoes. One of them, Elizabeth, knew the rules, had a very forceful personality and dominated the game; the other girl, Susan, just made pretty patterns with her pictures; the boy Philip in his quiet way was quite prepared to play the game, but found it hard to cope with Elizabeth's steam-roller tactics. She kept up a monologue. 'You need double clock to start. Who's got double clock? I have. I start.' Susan was the first to leave the table. She just wandered away, then Philip gave up cooperating and played his own game at his end of the table. Oblivious to this at first, Elizabeth went on playing. Then she too retired into her own game. To each child it was his own game and not something to cooperate in with the others. They just weren't ready.

All aspects of development, physical, intellectual and emotional, merge in play. The type of play and its role in the child's activities develops with age and maturity but at no stage does it deserve the somewhat derogatory implication in that familiar adult remark: 'He's *just* playing.'

More about Penguins
and Pelicans

Penguinews, which appears every month, contains details of all the new books issued by Penguins as they are published. From time to time it is supplemented by *Penguins in Print*, which is a complete list of all available books published by Penguins. (There are well over four thousand of these.)

A specimen copy of *Penguinews* will be sent to you free on request. For a year's issues (including the complete lists) please send 30p if you live in the United Kingdom, or 60p if you live elsewhere. Just write to Dept EP, Penguin Books Ltd, Harmondsworth, Middlesex, enclosing a cheque or postal order, and your name will be added to the mailing list.

Note: *Penguinews* and *Penguins in Print* are not available in the U.S.A. or Canada

Child Care
and the Growth of Love

John Bowlby

In 1951, under the auspices of the World Health Organization, Dr John Bowlby wrote a report on *Maternal Care and Mental Health* which collated expert world opinion on the subject and the issues arising from it – the prevention of juvenile and adult delinquency, the problem of the 'unwanted child', the training of women for motherhood, and the best ways of supplying the needs of children deprived of their natural mothers. This Pelican is a summary of Dr Bowlby's report, freed from many of its technicalities and prepared for the general reader.

This revised edition contains chapters based on an article by Dr Mary Salter Ainsworth, written in 1962 also for the World Health Organization when it once again made an important study of child care.

'It is a convenient and scholarly summary of evidence of the effects upon children of lack of personal attention, and it presents to administrators, social workers, teachers and doctors a reminder of the significance of the family' – *The Times*

The Child, The Family and The Outside World

D. W. Winnicott

Long clinical experience gave Dr Winnicott a unique standing in child psychiatry and few experts did more to present the world of children and parents to the general public.

Beginning at the natural bond between mother and child – the bond we call love, which is the key to personality – Dr Winnicott deals in turn in this volume with the phases of mother/infant, parent/child, and child/school. From the problems – which are not really problems – of feeding, weaning, and innate morality in babies, he ranges to the very real difficulties of only children, of stealing and lying, and of first experiments in independence. Shyness, sex education in schools, and the roots of agression are among the many other topics the author covers in a book which, for its manner of imparting knowledge simply and sympathetically, must be indispensable for intelligent parents.

'His style is lucid, his manner friendly, and his years of experience provide much wise insight into child behaviour and parental attitudes' – *British Journal of Psychology*